Steve Wilkinson

Karen Frazier

Barbara Hoskins

Ritsuko Nakata

OXFORD

UNIVERSITY PRESS

Let's Talk

A. Fill in the blanks.

Name	Age	Brothers and Sisters	Best Friend	Likes to
Tara	10			read
Clare	11		Sue	play the piano
		no brothers or sisters	Scott	

My name is Tara. I'm ____ years old. I have one brother. My best friend is Jenny.
I like to _____.

My name is Clare. I'm ____ years old. I have two sisters. My best friend is _____.
I like to _____.

My name is Matt. I'm 11 years old. I don't have any _____. My best friend is Scott. I like to play computer games.

B. Answer the questions.

Use the information on page 2.

1. How old is Tara? _____

2. Does Matt have any brothers? _____

3. What does Tara like to do? _____

4. Who has one brother? _____

5. Who likes to play the piano? _____

6. Who is Matt's best friend? _____

C. True or false? Check the answer.

1. Matt likes to play computer games. ☐ True   ☐ False

2. Clare has one brother and one sister. ☐ True   ☐ False

3. Clare's best friend is Jenny. ☐ True   ☐ False

4. Tara likes to read. ☐ True   ☐ False

5. Matt does not have any brothers or sisters. ☐ True   ☐ False

6. Tara's best friend is Scott. ☐ True   ☐ False

D. What about you?

Draw a picture and write about yourself.

Me

My name is _____

_____

_____

_____

A. Look at the chart and answer the questions.

	Monday	Tuesday	Wednesday
Jack	soccer ball	baseball glove and bat	basketball hoop
Sherri	laundry basket	table tennis	tent
June	towel	newspaper	fishing rod
Steve	computer	dog eating	bicycle

(Today — Tuesday)

1. Today Jack is playing baseball. What did he do yesterday?

_____

2. Yesterday Sherri went shopping. What is she doing today?

_____

3. Tomorrow June is going to go fishing. What did she do yesterday?

_____

4. Yesterday Steve played computer games. What is he going to do tomorrow?

_____

B. Match the questions and answers.

1. What does he like to do? •

2. What does she want to be? •

3. What is she going to do tomorrow? •

4. What do they have to do? •

5. What did he do yesterday? •

6. What does he have to do? •

• He played basketball.

• She is going to go swimming.

• They have to do their homework.

• He has to clean up his room.

• He likes to play computer games.

• She wants to be a veterinarian.

C. What about you?

1. What did you do yesterday? _____

_____

2. What are you going to do tomorrow?_____

_____

D. Answer the questions.

1. What does Shawn have to do?

   He has to do his homework.

2. What does Nina have to do?

   _____

3. What does Patti have to do?

   _____

4. What do Carl and Kate have to do?

   _____

5. What does Bill like to do?

   He likes to ride his bicycle.

6. What does Jan like to do?

   _____

7. What does Mindy like to do?

   _____

8. What do Frank and Marta like to do?

   _____

E. What about you?

1. What do you have to do? _____

   _____

2. What do you like to do? _____

   _____

Let's Read

A. Fill in the blanks.

treats	during	grains	Someday
zookeepers	volunteered	veterinarian	taking care of

Karlie loves animals. _____ she

wants to be a _____. Last

year Karlie _____ at the zoo

_____ summer vacation. She learned

a lot about _____ animals.

Every day she helped the _____

feed the animals. Some of the animals ate

_____ and others ate meat.

Sometimes they gave the animals frozen fruit

_____ .

B. Check "True" or "False."

1. Karlie volunteered at the zoo last winter. ☐ True ☐ False

2. Zookeepers take care of animals. ☐ True ☐ False

3. Some of the animals ate vegetables. ☐ True ☐ False

4. The animals sometimes ate frozen fruit treats. ☐ True ☐ False

C. Unscramble the words.

1. e e k p r o o e z s _____ 2. m a y s d o e _____

3. z e f o n r _____ 4. t a r t e s _____

5. i r u g d n _____ 6. u e e t r e v d l n o _____

7. s g r i n a _____ 8. a g t k i n a e r c f o_____

D. Find and circle the words.

snail	smear	small	snack	snow	smile

h	g	p	t	w	s	m	e	a	r	j	q	l
s	d	f	z	b	l	n	k	s	g	v	x	p
s	n	a	c	k	p	b	a	l	w	d	c	m
k	c	o	z	r	j	s	m	i	l	e	h	v
a	s	p	w	x	s	m	a	l	l	g	n	b

E. Look at the picture and fill in the blanks.

The _____ ate a _____ in the

_____ .

A. Match and connect. Fill in the blanks.

a coach

an engineer

a veterinarian

1.

Debra likes to take care of animals.

She wants to be _____

2.

Meg likes to play volleyball.

_____

3.

Jane likes to build models.

_____

B. Complete the sentences.

1. She doesn't want to be an engineer.

   She wants to be _____ a veterinarian.

2. _____ a teacher.

   _____ a coach.

3. _____ a baker.

   _____ an engineer.

4. _____ a coach.

   _____ a nurse.

C. What about you?

I want to be a _____ .   I don't want to be a _____ .

Write the questions.

1. _____

His name is Joe.

2. _____

He is 11 years old.

3. _____

Yes, he does. He has one brother.

4. _____

His best friend is Bob.

5. _____

He likes to collect stamps.

6. _____

He has to clean his room.

7. _____

He played soccer yesterday.

8. _____

He is going to go hiking tomorrow.

A. Follow the directions and color.

1. Color Jim's hair red.
   Color his eyes green.

2. Color Kelly's hair blond.
   Color her eyes brown.

3. Color Pete's hair brown.
   Color his eyes blue.

4. Color Jake's hair gray.
   Color his eyes black.

5. Color Teresa's hair black.
   Color her eyes blue.

Kelly

Jake

Pete

Teresa

Jim

B. Answer the questions.

Use the information above to answer the questions.

1. What does Pete look like? <u>He has brown hair and blue eyes.</u>

2. What does Kelly look like? _____

3. Does Jake have red hair? _____

4. Does Teresa have blue eyes? _____

5. Who has red hair? _____

6. Who has brown eyes? _____

C. What about you?

1. What do you look like? _____

2. What does your friend look like? _____

D. Color the hair and eyes.

Use the information from the chart below.

Paul

Peter (brother)

Patty (sister)

Bill (father)

Amy (mother)

	Hair Style	Hair Color	Eye Color	Glasses
Bill	short	brown	brown	yes
Peter	curly	blond	blue	no
Patty	long	black	black	yes
Amy	straight	red	green	no

E. Answer the questions.

Use the information above.

1. What does Paul's sister look like? <u>She has long black hair and black eyes. She wears glasses.</u>

2. What does Paul's father look like? _____

3. What does Paul's brother look like? _____

4. What does Paul's mother look like? _____

5. Does Paul's brother wear glasses? _____

6. Does Paul's father have curly hair? _____

Let's Learn

A. Write the names.
Use the information below.

1. Pete is the boy in the T-shirt and jeans.

2. Rob is the boy with glasses and short hair.

3. Ben is the boy in the T-shirt and baseball cap.

4. Matt is the boy with glasses and long hair.

5. Davy is the boy in the jeans and sweater.

_____ _____ _____ _____ _____

B. Answer the questions.
Use the information above.

1. What is Ben wearing?

_____

2. Is Pete wearing a T-shirt?

_____

3. Does Rob have long hair?

_____

4. Is Matt the boy with glasses and short hair?

_____

5. Is Davy the boy in the jeans and sweater?

_____

6. Is Pete the boy in the jeans and T-shirt?

_____

C. Look at the picture. Fill in the blanks. Make sentences.

Mike   Lori   Joan   Rod   Anna   Katie   Nick   Kim   Curtis

1. Katie's younger sister is the girl with the long hair.

   _____ is Katie's younger sister.

2. Katie's uncle is the man with glasses.

   _____ is Katie's uncle.

3. Katie's aunt is the woman in the small hat.

   _____ is Katie's aunt.

4. Katie's brother is the boy in the T-shirt and jeans.

   _____ is Katie's brother.

5. _____

   Joan is Katie's mother.

6. _____

   Curtis is Katie's cousin.

7. _____

   Rod is Katie's father.

8. _____

   Kim is Katie's older sister.

Let's Read

A. Find and circle the words.

| father | grandparents | family | uncle | aunt | mother |

k	c	t	z	r	j	s	f	a	m	i	l	y	w
s	g	r	a	n	d	p	a	r	e	n	t	s	c
h	g	p	u	n	c	l	e	a	r	j	q	l	a
a	s	p	n	x	f	a	t	h	e	r	b	b	d
j	m	o	t	h	e	r	a	l	w	d	c	m	g

B. Unscramble the words. Fill in the blanks.

This is Susan. She has a small _____ . She lives with her

                 a f m y l i

_____ and _____ . They live in an apartment.

    o h m r e t   t f r a e h

Susan's _____ and _____ live in a house next door.

      l e c n u   t u a n

Her _____ live far away.

    t n r d g a r n p a e s

C. Check "True" or "False."
Use the information above.

1. Susan has a big family.   ☐ True   ☐ False

2. Susan lives with her mother and father.   ☐ True   ☐ False

3. Susan lives in a house.   ☐ True   ☐ False

4. Susan's aunt and uncle live next door.   ☐ True   ☐ False

5. Susan's grandparents live next door.   ☐ True   ☐ False

D. Answer the questions.

1. Do you live in a house or an apartment?

_____

2. Do you have a big family or a small family?

_____

3. Who do you live with?

_____

4. Do your grandparents live far away?

_____

5. Do you have any cousins? How many?

_____

6. Do you have any aunts or uncles? How many?

_____

7. Who lives next door?

_____

E. Write the words and draw the pictures.

1.  - an + ing =

_____

2.  -s + t - g + s =

_____

Let's Chant

A. Which word is different?
Circle one word in each box.

1. | (skirt) | hair | eyes | nose | mouth |

2. | black | green | brown | gray | tall |

3. | tall | brown | short | thin | fat |

4. | curly | straight | long | young | blond |

5. | shirt | bat | dress | T-shirt | pants |

6. | mother | brother | sister | teacher | father |

B. Add three words of your own to each list.

1. socks   hat   _____   _____   _____

2. blond   brown   _____   _____   _____

3. grandfather   uncle   _____   _____   _____

4. woman   baby   _____   _____   _____

C. Choose a title for each list.

| Clothes | Hair Style | Eye Color | Family |

aunt	shoes	brown	long
cousin	cap	blue	curly
grandfather	gloves	green	straight
brother	sweater	black	short

D. Unscramble the answers.

1. Who's that?

mother   the   my   That's   hair   with   curly

_____

2. Who's that?

cap   father   the   in   That's   baseball   my

_____

A. Unscramble the answers and label the picture.

1. Which man is Todd's father?

   the with man He glasses is

   _____

2. Which woman is Todd's mother?

   hat woman is She the the in

   _____

3. Which man is Todd's uncle?

   the in is the man He jeans

   _____

4. Which woman is Todd's aunt?

   in is She dress the woman the

   _____

Todd's _____

Todd's _____

Todd

Todd's _____

Todd's _____

B. Match the questions and answers.
Use the picture of Todd's family.

1. What does Todd's father look like? •

2. What does Todd's mother look like? •

3. What does Todd's aunt look like? •

4. What does Todd's uncle look like? •

• She is short and she has long curly hair.

• He is tall and he is wearing jeans.

• She is tall and she has long straight hair.

• He is tall and he has short curly hair.

Let's Review

A. Write the questions.

1. Steve: _____

   Jane: My name is Jane.

2. Steve: _____

   Jane: I'm eleven years old.

3. Steve: _____

   Jane: I like to read books.

4. Steve: _____

   Jane: My best friend is Sherri.

5. Steve: _____

   _____

   Jane: Yes, I do. I have one brother.

6. Steve: _____

   _____

   Jane: My brother's name is Mark.

B. Answer the questions.

1. Which boy is Amy's brother? <u>Her brother is the</u>
   <u>boy in the T-shirt and jeans.</u>

2. Which man is her uncle?_____

   _____

3. Which woman is her mother?_____

   _____

4. Which man is her father?_____

   _____

5. Which woman is her aunt?_____

   _____

Amy

mother   brother   father

aunt   uncle

C. Follow the directions.

Read the sentences below and color the eyes and hair.

Lori   Joan   Jake   Becky   Mary

1. Lori has green eyes and red hair.
2. Joan has gray hair and black eyes.
3. Becky has blond hair and blue eyes.
4. Mary has brown hair and brown eyes.

D. Write the names.

Read the sentences and look at the pictures above.
Fill in the names of Jake's aunt, sister, mother, and cousin.

1. Jake's sister has green eyes.
2. Jake's mother has short curly hair.
3. Jake's cousin has long curly hair.
4. Jake's aunt has long straight hair.

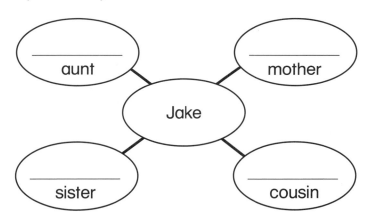

E. Fill in the blanks. Complete the crossword.

Use the information above.

1. Jake's _____ is the woman with
   brown hair and brown eyes.

2. Joan is the woman with long _____ hair.

3. Jake's sister is the girl with _____ eyes.

4. Becky is Jake's _____ .

A. Complete the conversations.
Use the words at the bottom of the page.

1.

Would _____ _____ _____ _____
    k   c   i   m

_____ _____ _____ _____ ?
    r   d   a   b

_____ , _____ _____ _____ _____ .
  j   e   n   m

2.

_____ _____ _____ _____
    k   c   i   m

_____ _____ _____ _____ ?
    r   f   a   o

_____ , _____ _____ _____ .
  l   p   g   h

3.

_____ _____ _____ _____
    k   c   i   m

_____ _____ _____ _____ ?
    r   s   a   o

_____ ! _____ _____ _____ .
  l   e   n   m

_____ _____ _____ _____ _____ _____ .
  q   r   w   t   v   u

a with   **b** me   **c** you   **d** swimming   **e** I'd   **f** fishing

g I   **h** can't   **i** like   **j** Sure   **k** Would   **l** Thanks

m to   **n** love   **o** us   **p** but   **q** I'll   **r** go

s camping   **t** ask   **u** parents   **v** my   **w** and

B. Match and connect. Answer the questions.

a backpack

a baseball

a towel

a bathing suit

a fishing pole

hiking boots

a tennis ball

bait

a mitt

a tennis racket

1. He is going to go fishing tomorrow.
   What will he need?

   He will need _____

   and _____

2. She is going to go swimming tomorrow.
   What will she need?

   _____

   _____

3. He is going to go hiking tomorrow.
   What will he need?

   _____

   _____

4. He is going to play baseball tomorrow.
   What will he need?

   _____

   _____

5. She is going to play tennis tomorrow.
   What will she need?

   _____

   _____

C. Fill in the blanks.

It will be hot tomorrow. Bob is going to go to the beach. What will he need?

1. *He will need* _____ a towel.   2. *He won't need* _____ mittens.

3. _____ a sweater.   4. _____ a bathing suit.

5. _____ a jacket.   6. _____ a coat.

A. Fill in the blanks.

do his homework   take a bath   read a book

have a picnic   go canoeing   play baseball

watch TV   play tennis

On Saturday morning John _____will play tennis_____. In the afternoon he

_____ and then he _____. In the

evening he _____.

B. Complete the calendar.

On Sunday morning John will go canoeing with his friends. In the afternoon they will have a picnic. In the evening he will take a bath and then he will read a book.

C. Look at the chart and answer the questions.

Tomorrow	morning	afternoon	evening
Jim			
Sally			
Jennifer			
Greg and Pete			

1. What will Jim do tomorrow morning?

   He will play baseball.

2. What will Sally do tomorrow afternoon?

   _____

3. What will Jennifer do tomorrow afternoon?

   _____

4. What will Greg and Pete do tomorrow morning?

   _____

5. Will Sally need binoculars tomorrow evening?

   _____

6. Will Jim need a paddle tomorrow afternoon?

   _____

7. Will Jennifer need a backpack tomorrow evening?

   _____

8. Will Greg and Pete need hiking boots tomorrow evening?

   _____

D. What about you?

1. What will you do tomorrow morning?

   _____

2. What will you do tomorrow afternoon?

   _____

3. What will you do tomorrow evening?

   _____

A. Look at the code. Write the words.

Code																									
a	b	c	d	e	f	g	h	i	j	k	l	m	n	o	p	q	r	s	t	u	v	w	x	y	z
↓	↓	↓	↓	↓	↓	↓	↓	↓	↓	↓	↓	↓	↓	↓	↓	↓	↓	↓	↓	↓	↓	↓	↓	↓	↓
z	a	b	c	d	e	f	g	h	i	j	k	l	m	n	o	p	q	r	s	t	u	v	w	x	y

Example: d b u = cat

1. m f b w f t = <u>leaves</u>

2. q b q f s = _____

3. q b j o u = _____

4. x b j u = _____

5. h m v f = _____

6. q b j o u c s v t i = _____

B. Fill in the blanks.

Use the words above. You will use some words more than once.

You will need <u>leaves</u>, a _____, _____, _____, and glue. First, _____

the _____ onto the paper. _____ for an hour. Then _____ over the leaves and

the _____. Let the paint dry. Then carefully take the leaves off the _____.

C. Make a code. Write code words.

Look at the pattern and continue the code. Then use the code.

Code																									
a	b	c	d	e	f	g	h	i	j	k	l	m	n	o	p	q	r	s	t	u	v	w	x	y	z
↓	↓	↓	↓	↓	↓	↓	↓	↓	↓	↓	↓	↓	↓	↓	↓	↓	↓	↓	↓	↓	↓	↓	↓	↓	↓
<u>z</u>	<u>y</u>	<u>x</u>	<u>w</u>	<u>v</u>	<u>u</u>	_	_	_	_	_	_	_	_	_	_	_	_	_	_	_	_	<u>d</u>	<u>c</u>	<u>b</u>	<u>a</u>

1. <u>h s z k v g</u> = shapes

2. _____ = wrapping paper

3. _____ = beautiful

4. _____ = birthday card

5. _____ = pattern

6. _____ = different

D. Write the words and complete the crossword.

Across

1.

2.

3.

4.

Down

1.

2.

3.

E. Check John's answers. Correct the mistakes.

Spelling Test   John

1. ~~schunk~~   **skunk**
2. skeleton
3. skool
4. skedule
5. skate
6. scholars
7. skirt

A. Unscramble and write.

1.

i r a y n

_____

2.

n n y u s

_____

3.

y w n i d

_____

4.

c u o l y d

_____

5.

n y w s o

_____

B. Write the answers.

How will the weather be tomorrow?

1. It will be rainy and cold tomorrow.

2. _____

_____

3. _____

_____

4. _____

_____

C. Complete the sentences.

I will need   I won't need

1. It will be rainy and cold tomorrow. I will need _____ an umbrella.

2. It will be snowy and cold tomorrow. _____ boots.

3. It will be sunny and hot tomorrow. _____ a coat.

4. It will be windy and cold tomorrow. _____ a coat.

Let's Listen

A. Write two things you need for each activity.

1. go swimming   <u>towel, bathing suit</u>   2. play baseball   _____

3. paint a picture   _____   4. go camping   _____

5. play tennis   _____   6. write a letter   _____

7. go hiking   _____   8. go fishing   _____

B. Fill in the blanks.

1. Carl <u>will need</u> _____

   and _____.

2. Kate <u>will need</u> _____

   _____.

3. Dave and Sam _____

   _____.

4. Kristy_____

   _____.

C. Write the answers.
Use the information above.

1. What will Kate do tomorrow?   2. What will Dave and Sam do tomorrow?

_____   _____

3. What will Kristy do tomorrow?   4. Will Carl go fishing tomorrow?

_____   _____

5. Will Kristy play tennis tomorrow?   6. Will Dave and Sam play baseball tomorrow?

_____   _____

Let's Talk

A. Unscramble the subjects.

Jenny's Schedule

Monday	Tuesday	Wednesday
E g h l s i n	t r a	t m a h
c e s e i c n	y i t s r h o	e g o r g h a y p
t r i a l e r u e t	h i y p l a c s	c s m i u
	c u d e t a n i o	

B. Look at the chart and fill in the blanks.

	John	Carol	Mark
Is geography easy for you?	yes	yes	no
Is math easy for you?	no	yes	yes
Is science easy for you?	yes	yes	yes
Is English easy for you?	yes	no	yes

1. _____ is hard for Mark. 2. _____ is hard for Carol.

3. Science _____ John. 4. Math _____ John.

C. Fill in the blanks. Find and circle the words.

1. easy → <u>easier</u>

2. hard → _____

3. big → _____

4. small → _____

5. fast → _____

6. slow → _____

7. tall → _____

8. short → _____

s	s	z	e	t	f	b	h	t
h	l	m	v	a	h	h	a	a
o	o	g	a	j	s	k	r	l
r	w	j	s	l	v	i	d	l
t	e	r	w	h	l	x	e	e
e	r	b	i	g	g	e	r	r
r	q	f	a	s	t	e	r	s

D. Complete the sentences.
Use the chart on page 28.

1. John thinks geography <u>is easy.</u>

   He <u>thinks geography is easier than</u> _____ math.

2. Mark thinks math _____

   He _____ geography.

3. Carol thinks English _____

   She _____ science.

4. John thinks math _____

   He _____ English.

E. What about you?

1. Which subject is easier, math or English?

   _____

2. Which subject is harder, history or geography?

   _____

Let's Learn

A. Fill in the blanks.

1.

big   bigger   the biggest

2.

_____   smaller   _____

3.

fast   _____   _____

4.

_____   _____   the slowest

5.

_____   taller   _____

6.

short   _____   _____

B. Look at the pictures above. Make sentences.

1. The caterpillar _is slower than the snake._

    The caterpillar _is faster than the snail._

2. The horse _____

    The horse _____

3. The cat _____

    The cat _____

4. The car _____

    The car _____

C. Look at the pictures. Answer the questions.

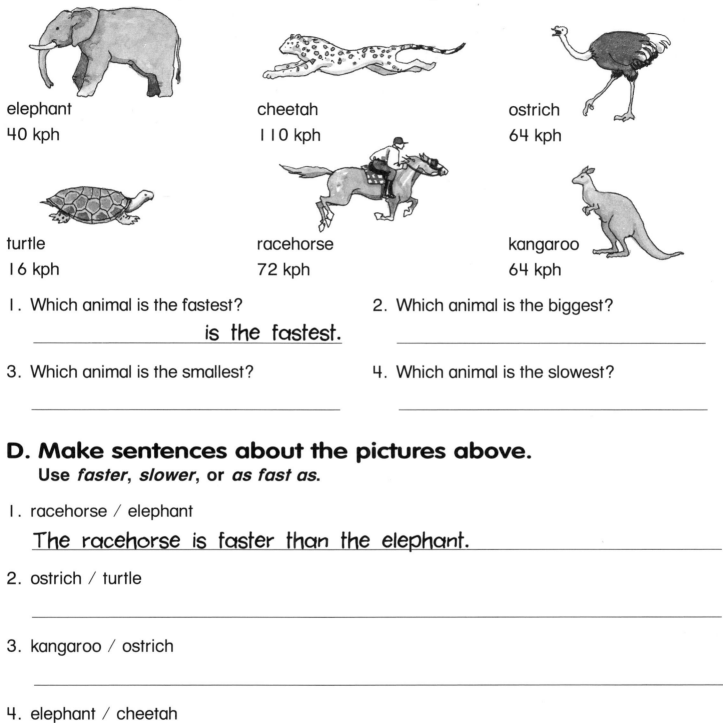

elephant
40 kph

cheetah
110 kph

ostrich
64 kph

turtle
16 kph

racehorse
72 kph

kangaroo
64 kph

1. Which animal is the fastest?

_____ is the fastest.

2. Which animal is the biggest?

_____

3. Which animal is the smallest?

_____

4. Which animal is the slowest?

_____

D. Make sentences about the pictures above.
   Use *faster*, *slower*, or *as fast as*.

1. racehorse / elephant

   The racehorse is faster than the elephant.

2. ostrich / turtle

   _____

3. kangaroo / ostrich

   _____

4. elephant / cheetah

   _____

5. racehorse / kangaroo

   _____

A. Complete the story.
Use the key to fill in the blanks.

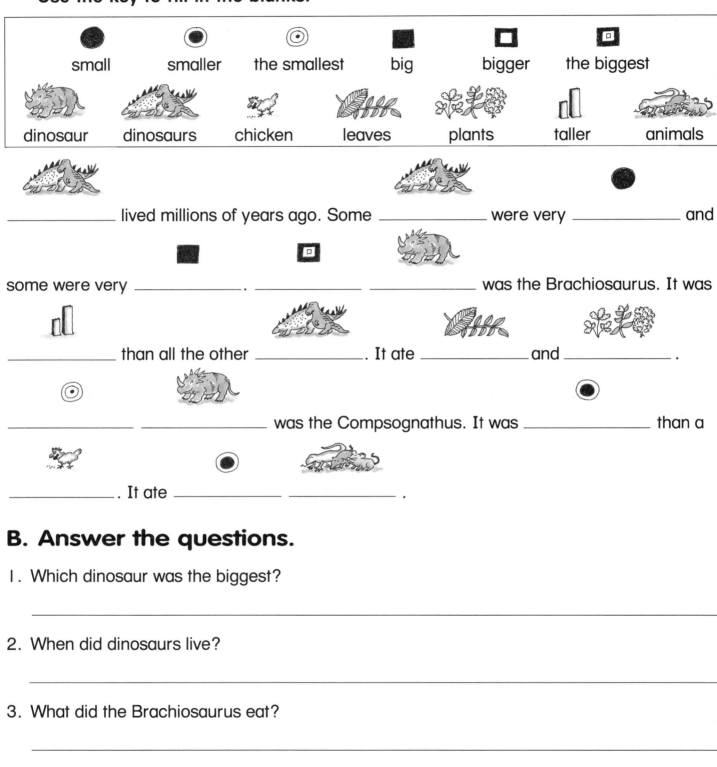

small   smaller   the smallest   big   bigger   the biggest

dinosaur   dinosaurs   chicken   leaves   plants   taller   animals

_____ lived millions of years ago. Some _____ were very _____ and

some were very _____. _____ _____ was the Brachiosaurus. It was

_____ than all the other _____. It ate _____ and _____.

_____ _____ was the Compsognathus. It was _____ than a

_____. It ate _____ _____.

B. Answer the questions.

1. Which dinosaur was the biggest?

   _____

2. When did dinosaurs live?

   _____

3. What did the Brachiosaurus eat?

   _____

4. Did the Compsognathus eat plants?

   _____

C. Check "True" or "False."
Look at the story on page 32.

1. The Brachiosaurus ate small animals. ☐ True ☐ False

2. The Compsognathus was the smallest dinosaur. ☐ True ☐ False

3. Dinosaurs lived millions of years ago. ☐ True ☐ False

4. The Compsognathus ate leaves and plants. ☐ True ☐ False

D. Fill in the blanks.
Use the words and phrases in the box. Use each one only once.

Compsognathus	millions of years ago	biggest	animals

1. The _____ dinosaur was the Brachiosaurus.

2. The _____ was smaller than a chicken.

3. Dinosaurs lived _____.

4. The Compsognathus ate smaller _____.

E. Circle and write.

1.  st   str
_____

2. st   str
_____

3. st   str
_____

4. st   str
_____

5.  st   str
_____

6. st   str
_____

F. Read and draw.

The stork ate strawberries in the stream.

Let's Sing

A. Write the animals from longest to shortest.

A crocodile is longer than a cobra.

A python is longer than a crocodile.

A cobra is longer than a lizard.

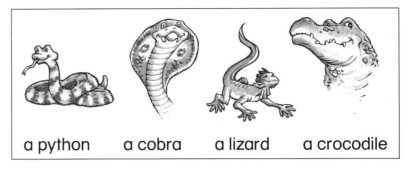

a python   a cobra   a lizard   a crocodile

1. _____   2. _____   3. _____   4. _____

   the longest   the shortest

B. Write the animals from biggest to smallest.

A beetle is bigger than a bee.

A fly is bigger than a flea.

A bee is bigger than a fly.

a fly   a bee   a beetle   a flea

1. _____   2. _____   3. _____   4. _____

   the biggest   the smallest

C. Write the animals from fastest to slowest.

A hippopotamus is faster than a turtle.

An elephant is faster than a hippopotamus.

An ostrich is faster than an elephant.

an elephant   a turtle   a hippopotamus   an ostrich

1. _____   2. _____   3. _____   4. _____

   the fastest   the slowest

A. Answer the questions.

THE **SPEEDO!**
(120 kph)

THE **TURBO!**
(150 kph)

THE **SLUGGO!**
(80 kph)

THE **NIFTY!**
(120 kph)

1. Which car is the fastest?
   _____ is the fastest.

2. Which car is the smallest?
   _____

3. Which car is the biggest?
   _____

4. Which car is the slowest?
   _____

B. Fill in the blanks. Use the picture above.

1. _____ is slower than the Speedo.   2. _____ is as fast as _____.

3. The Speedo is _____ the Turbo.   4. The Nifty is _____ the Sluggo.

C. Look at the chart. Fill in the blanks.

	English	**math**	**Science**	**art**
James	easy	easy	hard	hard
Carrie	hard	hard	easy	easy

1. Math is _____ for James.

2. Science is _____ for James.

3. English is _____ for Carrie.

4. James thinks art is _____ than math.

5. Carrie thinks science is _____ than English.

6. Carrie thinks math is _____ than science.

Let's Review

A. Write the questions.

1. Jason is going to go swimming. What will he need?

_____

2. Lee is going to draw a picture. What will she need?

_____

3. Nick and Dave are going to play baseball. What will they need?

_____

4. Marsha is going to go hiking. What will she need?

_____

B. Look at the chart. Answer the questions.

	Saturday morning	Saturday afternoon	Saturday evening
John	dentist	soccer	homework
Sara	piano	shopping	TV
Bob	fishing	tennis	movie

1. What will John do on Saturday evening?

_____

2. What will Sara do on Saturday morning?

_____

3. Who will watch TV on Saturday evening?

_____

4. Who will go to the dentist on Saturday morning?

_____

5. Will Bob need a fishing pole on Saturday morning?

_____

6. Will John need a tennis racket on Saturday afternoon?

_____

C. Complete the sentences.

1.
   History is easy, but English is hard.

   He thinks history **is easier than English.**

2.
   Science is hard, but geography is easy.

   She thinks science _____

   _____

3.
   English is hard, but math is easy.

   She thinks math _____

   _____

4.
   Math is easy, but history is hard.

   He thinks history _____

   _____

D. Circle the correct word. Fill in the blanks.

1. fast	faster	fastest

The cheetah is the _____ animal on land.

2. slow	slower	slowest

A turtle is _____ than a horse.

3. big	bigger	biggest

The elephant is the _____ animal on land.

4. small	smaller	smallest

A dog is _____ than an ostrich.

E. Read the sentences. Answer the question.

A kangaroo is faster than a cat. A fox is as fast as a kangaroo.

Is a fox faster than a cat? _____

F. Read the sentences. Fill in the names.

Andy was faster than Ted.

Ed was the fastest.

David was slower than Ted.

Mike was the slowest.

1 _____
2 _____
3 _____
4 _____
5 _____

Let's Talk

A. Match the questions and answers.

1.   Why does Mike like summer best? •   • Because she likes planting flowers.

2.   Why does Mary like spring best? •   • Because she likes skiing.

3.   Why does James like fall best? •   • Because he likes waterskiing.

4.   Why does Elizabeth like winter best? •   • Because he likes jumping into leaves.

B. Answer the questions.

1. Why does Pete like spring best? _He likes spring_ _best because_ _____

2. Why does Pam like summer best? _____

_____

3. Why does Betty like fall best? _____

_____

4. Why does John like winter best? _____

_____

C. Fill in the blanks. Complete the crossword.

Across

1. Bob likes _____ best because he likes swimming.

2. Susan likes _____ best because she likes skiing.

3. Shanta likes winter best because she likes _____ skating.

4. Ben likes fall best because he likes _____ football.

Down

1. Donna's favorite _____ is summer because she likes waterskiing.

2. Janet likes _____ best because she likes planting flowers.

3. Blake likes spring because he likes flying _____ .

4. Jim's favorite season is _____ because he likes jumping into leaves.

D. What about you?

What do you like doing in the different seasons?

Example: <u>In spring I like planting flowers.</u>

Spring: _____   Summer: _____

_____   _____

Fall: _____   Winter: _____

_____   _____

A. Fill in the chart.

today	next month	tomorrow	next week	last month	yesterday
last week	next year	last year	this week	this year	this month

	past	now	future
day		today	
week			next week
month		this month	
year	last year		

B. Write today's date and answer the questions.

Today is _____.

            day   month   date   year

1. What month was last month?

_____

3. What month is next month?

_____

5. What year was last year?

_____

2. What year is this year?

_____

4. What year is next year?

_____

6. What month is this month?

_____

C. Fill in the blanks with "Last" or "Next."

1. _____ summer Kate went to math camp.

2. _____ year Brian is going to go to a dude ranch.

3. _____ week Bob and Mary are going to go to the beach.

4. _____ winter Sue learned how to ice-skate.

5. _____ Sunday Jake is going to clean his room.

6. _____ month Kathy went to see her grandparents.

D. Fill in the blanks with "went" or "is going to go."

1. Last week Tom and Bill _____ fishing.

2. Next winter Jodi _____ skiing.

3. Last month Ken _____ waterskiing.

4. Last Saturday Julie _____ ice-skating.

5. Tomorrow Sarah _____ shopping.

6. Next summer Ann _____ to camp.

E. Correct the sentences.
Each of the following sentences has one wrong word. Draw a line through the wrong word. Then write the correct word.

1. ~~Last~~ *Next* summer we are going to go to our grandparents' house.

2. Next week we had tests at school.

3. Tomorrow I went to the dentist.

4. Last month Joe is going to have a birthday party.

5. Next summer I learned how to ride a horse.

6. Yesterday I am going to a museum.

A. Fill in the blanks to complete the story.

| winter vacation | ice-skating | June | skiing | snowy | lives | cold |

Jeff _____ in New Zealand. In _____ it is winter there. It is _____ and _____.
During _____ Jeff goes _____ and _____.

B. Answer the questions. Use the story above.

1. Where does Jeff live?

_____

2. What season is it in New Zealand in June?

_____

3. Is it hot and sunny in New Zealand in June?

_____

4. What does Jeff do in winter?

_____

C. Write a story.
Use the words in the box to write a story about Maria. Follow the model above.

| Maria | Brazil | December | summer |
| hot and sunny | summer vacation | swimming | sailing |

_____

_____

_____

_____

_____

D. What about you?

1. Is it summer in your country in June?

_____

2. What can you do in your country in the summer?

_____

3. What can you do in your country in the winter?

_____

4. In your country, which months are summer? Which months are winter?

   Write the months.

   winter   _____   _____   _____

   spring   _____   _____   _____

   summer   _____   _____   _____

   fall   _____   _____   _____

E. Answer the quiz questions.
Choose the answers from the word box. You do not need to use every word.

| quiz   question   queen   squeeze   square   squid |

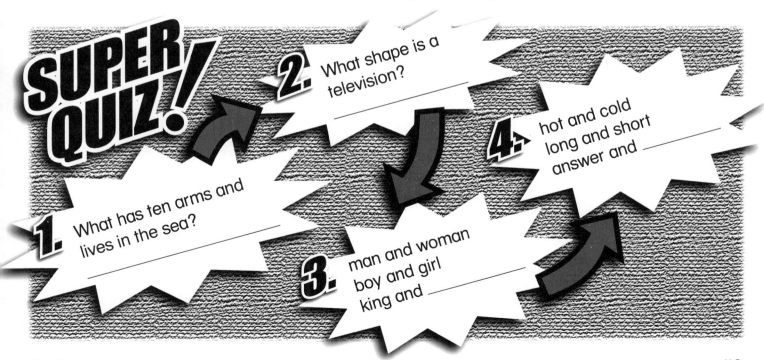

SUPER QUIZ!

1. What has ten arms and lives in the sea?

_____

2. What shape is a television?

_____

3. man and woman
boy and girl
king and _____

4. hot and cold
long and short
answer and _____

Let's Chant

A. Answer the questions.

Last Year   Liz   Next Year

1. Where did Liz go last winter?

   _____

2. Where did Liz go last summer?

   _____

3. What did she buy in London?

   _____

4. Did she buy anything in Paris?

   _____

5. Where is Liz going to go next winter?

   _____

6. Where is Liz going to go next summer?

   _____

7. What is Liz going to do in Hawaii?

   _____

8. What is Liz going to do in Canada?

   _____

B. Complete the crossword puzzle.
Use the information above to fill in the blanks.

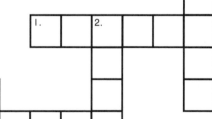

Across

1. Next winter Liz is going to be in _____ .

2. In Paris Liz _____ a T-shirt.

Down

1. _____ winter Liz went to London.

2. _____ summer Liz is going to go to Hawaii.

3. In Canada Liz is _____ to go skiing.

Let's Listen

A. Look at the chart. Fill in the blanks.

Name		Favorite Season	Likes	Vacation Last Year	Vacation Next Year
Steve		winter	skiing	Canada	dude ranch
Kay		summer	waterskiing	Hawaii	math camp
Erika		summer	swimming	beach	Australia
Shawn		winter	ice-skating	ski camp	zoo

1. Kay: My _____ is summer because

_____ .

2. Shawn: I like _____ best because

_____ .

3. Erika: My _____ is summer because

_____ .

4. Steve: I like _____ best because

_____ .

B. Answer the questions. Use the chart above.

1. Where did Kay go during vacation last year?

_____

2. Where is Erika going to go during vacation next year?

_____

3. What does Shawn like doing?

_____

4. When did Erika go to the beach?

_____

5. When is Steve going to go to a dude ranch?

_____

6. Did Kay go to Canada for vacation last year?

_____

Let's Talk

A. Look at the pictures. Make two lists.

sandwiches   carrots   milk   tomatoes

ice cream   potatoes   butter   cake

water   cookies   eggs   orange juice

You can't count   You can count

_____ _____   _____ _____

_____ _____   _____ _____

_____ _____   _____ _____

B. Make sentences about the pictures above.
Use *There is* and *There are*.

There is...   There are...

There is some ice cream.   There are some sandwiches.

C. What is in the refrigerator?

There is some cheese.

There are some apples.

D. Write the questions and answers.

1. What is in the cupboard?

2. _____

3. _____

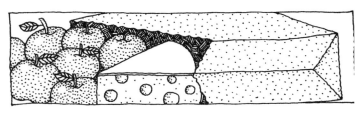

4. _____

A. Match the sentences and pictures.

1. There is a lot of spaghetti. •

2. There are a few bananas. •

3. There are a lot of bananas. •

4. There is a little spaghetti. •

B. Complete the sentences.

1. There is a lot of ___cake___ and a lot of ___juice___ .

2. There is a little _____ and a little _____ .

3. There are a lot of _____ and a lot of _____ .

4. There are a few _____ and a few _____ .

C. Make sentences.

Use *a little*, *a few*, or *a lot of*.

1. _____

_____

2. _____

_____

3. _____

_____

4. _____

_____

D. Write questions.

Use *How much* or *How many*.

1. How much ice cream is there?

There is a lot of ice cream.

2. _____

There are a lot of apples.

3. _____

There is a little bread.

4. _____

There is a lot of chicken.

5. _____

There are a few napkins.

E. Write questions and answers.

Use the information in the picture above.

1. pizza

_____

_____

2. plates

_____

_____

3. forks

_____

_____

4. cake

_____

_____

A. Complete the crossword puzzle.
Use the words in the box to fill in the blanks.

The food _____ can help you choose _____ food. You need
            (5)   (6)

to eat a lot of the food at the _____ and only a little of the food at the
                                  (2)

_____ . You need to eat a lot of _____ , like rice and bread, every
     (3)   (8)

day. You also need to eat a lot of _____ , like carrots and _____ .
                           (1)   (4)

Fruits, like apples and oranges, are good for you, too. You need to eat some

_____ every day. There is protein in milk, cheese, fish, and eggs.
   (7)

| healthy | vegetables | top | grains | pyramid | bottom | protein | spinach |

B. Make lists.
Look at the words in the box. Are these foods grains, vegetables, or fruits?
Write the words in three lists.

oranges   spinach   carrots   bread   rice   apples

Grains	Vegetables	Fruits
_____	_____	_____
_____	_____	_____

C. What about you?

1. What did you eat for dinner last night? Write the food names next to the correct food group.

   grains: _____

   vegetables: _____

   fruits: _____

   protein: _____

2. What is your favorite fruit? _____

3. What is your favorite vegetable? _____

D. Complete the crossword puzzle.
Use three words from the word box.

spring   splash   spruce   splish   sprout   splatter

1. The name of a tree

2. The season before summer

3. A young plant or flower

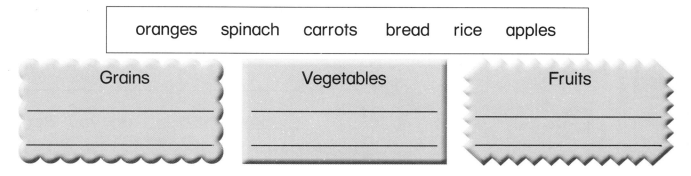

Let's Chant

Use the code.

For the questions, write *How much* or *How many*. Use the code to answer each question. Then circle the matching picture.

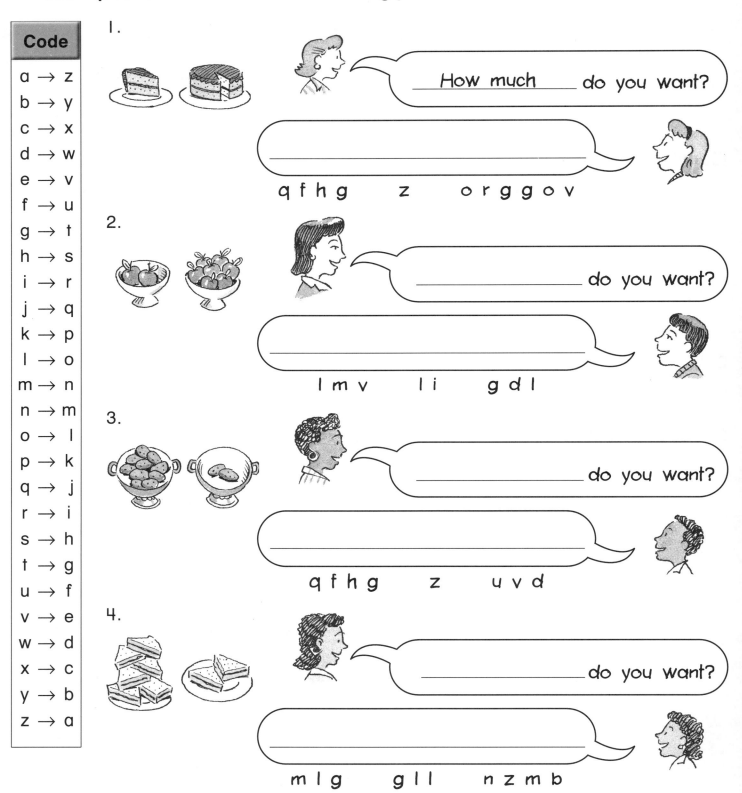

Code
a → z
b → y
c → x
d → w
e → v
f → u
g → t
h → s
i → r
j → q
k → p
l → o
m → n
n → m
o → l
p → k
q → j
r → i
s → h
t → g
u → f
v → e
w → d
x → c
y → b
z → a

1.

How much   do you want?

q f h g   z   o r g g o v

2.

_____ do you want?

l m v   l i   g d l

3.

_____ do you want?

q f h g   z   u v d

4.

_____ do you want?

m l g   g l l   n z m b

Let's Listen

A. What is on the picnic table?

Complete the sentences. Then draw the food in the picture.

1. __There are__ a few apples and __there is__ a lot of chicken.

2. _____ a lot of cookies and _____ a little cake.

3. _____ a little orange juice and _____ a lot of sandwiches.

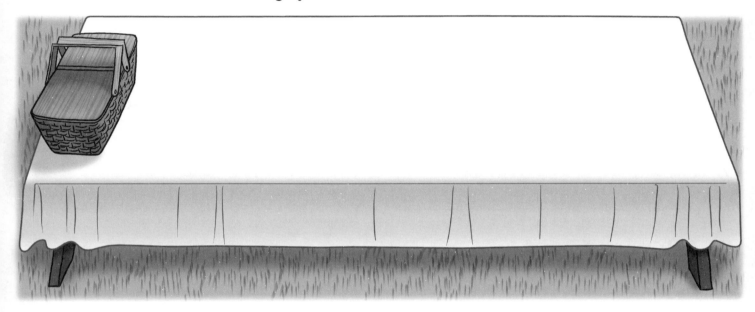

B. Correct the mistakes.

Each question or answer below has one mistake. Put a line through the word and write the correct word.

1. How ~~much~~ *many* apples are there?

   There are a lot of apples.

2. How many cookies are there?

   There is a few cookies.

3. How much cake are there?

   There is a little cake.

4. How many napkins are there?

   There are a little napkins.

5. How much soda is there?

   There is a few soda.

6. How many peaches are there?

   There is a lot of peaches.

7. How many milk is there?

   There is a little milk.

8. How much bananas are there?

   There are a few bananas.

A. Answer the questions.

1. How old were you last year?

   _____

2. How old will you be next year?

   _____

3. What grade were you in last year?

   _____

4. What grade are you in now?

   _____

5. What grade will you be in next year?

   _____

6. What did you do last winter?

   _____

7. What will you do next winter?

   _____

8. What is your favorite season?

   _____

9. What do you like to do in summer?

   _____

10. What do you like to do in winter?

    _____

B. Ask your friend.
Now ask your friend the same questions. Write the answers.

My friend's name is _____

1. Last year _____ was _____ years old.
2. _____
3. _____
4. _____
5. _____
6. _____
7. _____
8. _____
9. _____
10. _____

C. Make sentences and draw.

Make your own sentences. Use *a lot of, a little,* or *a few.*
Then draw a picture.

	1. bananas

_____

_____

	2. salad

_____

_____

	3. milk

_____

_____

	4. hamburgers

_____

_____

D. Write questions and answers.

Use *How much* and *How many*. Then answer the questions and circle the matching picture.

1. cookies

How many cookies
are there? There are
a lot of cookies.

2. rice

_____

_____

_____

3. milk

_____

_____

_____

4. carrots

_____

_____

_____

5. peaches

_____

_____

_____

6. cake

_____

_____

_____

Let's Talk

A. Fill in the blanks.

1. <u>This is</u> John <u>when he was</u> <u>two years old.</u>

2. _____ Amanda _____

_____

3. _____ Paul _____

_____

4. _____ Jane _____

_____

B. Write questions and answers.

Look at the pictures above. Write down a question and answer about each child.

1. <u>What did John want to be when he was two?</u>

<u>He wanted to be a firefighter.</u>

2. _____

_____

3. _____

_____

4. _____

_____

C. What about you?

What did you want to be when you were little?

_____

D. Answer the questions.
Judy's Photo Album

1. When did Judy learn how to do a somersault? She learned how to do a somersault when she was five.

2. When did she learn how to write her name? _____

3. When did she learn how to swim? _____

4. When did she learn how to ride a bike? _____

5. When did she learn how to walk? _____

6. When did she learn how to do a handstand? _____

E. What about you?

When did you learn how to write your name?

_____

A. Complete the sentences.

What were the children doing when the coach blew the whistle?

1. John <u>was doing his homework.</u>

2. Sara and Helen _____

3. Mike _____

4. Tom _____

5. Pete _____

6. Jake and Clyde _____

7. Charles _____

8. Wendy _____

B. Write two sentences for each picture.

1. Mary <u>was washing her hair when the</u> <u>doorbell rang.</u>
When <u>the doorbell rang, Mary was washing</u> <u>her hair.</u>

2. Steve and Nick _____

_____

When _____

_____

3. Lisa _____

_____

When _____

_____

4. Bob _____

_____

When _____

_____

5. June _____

_____

When _____

_____

Let's Read

A. Fill in the blanks.

Use the words in the box. You can use some words more than once.

| visit | family | homesick | During | homestay | English | American | often | enjoy |

Last winter, Li went on a h_____ to the United States. He lived with the

Wilson f_____. He went to school with his A_____ brother. At

first, speaking E_____ every day was very hard. Li was h_____. But

then he started to enjoy his h_____. Li liked living with the Wilsons.

D_____ winter vacation, they went skiing. Now Li is back home. He

o_____ writes to his A_____ friends. Next year the Wilsons are

going to v_____ Li in Taiwan.

B. Complete the sentences.

| homestay | homesick | vacation |

1. When you want to go home and see your own family, you are _____.

2. During _____, you do not go to school or work.

3. When you stay in another country with another family, you are on a _____.

C. Write a story.

Read about Li's homestay again. Then write a story about Yuki. Yuki is a Japanese girl. She went on a homestay to Australia.

last year	Australia	Walker family	Australian	sister
Yuki	English	summer	vacation	Australian	Japan	waterskiing

Last year, Yuki _____

_____

_____

_____

_____

_____

_____

D. Unscramble and write the words.

openh	kkcon	seenk	hamtnpo	slekcunk	ogppthoarh

1. _____

2. _____

3. _____

4. _____

5. _____

6. _____

——————————————— Let's Chant ——————————————

A. Answer the questions.

1. How old were you when you learned how to walk?

   I was _____ when I learned how to walk. ____

2. How old were you when you learned how to talk?

   _____

3. How old were you when you learned how to run?

   _____

4. How old were you when you learned how to do a cartwheel?

   _____

5. How old were you when you started to learn English?

   _____

6. How old were you when you learned how to ride a bike?

   _____

B. Think of two more questions.

1. How old were you when you _____?

   I was _____

2. How old were you when you _____?

   _____

C. Ask a friend.
Choose three questions from this page and ask a friend. Write the answers.

1. _____

2. _____

3. _____

A. Write the questions and answers.

5 years old

1. <u>When did she learn how to write her name?</u>
<u>She learned how to write her name when she was five.</u>

8 years old

2. _____
_____
_____
_____

9 years old

3. _____
_____
_____
_____

B. Look at the pictures and make sentences.

1. When <u>it started to rain,</u>
Greg <u>was riding his bike.</u>

2. When _____
Scott _____

3. Tom and Pete _____
when _____

4. Jenny _____
when _____

Let's Talk

A. Complete the questions. Write the answers.

1. _Has he ever been to_ Spain?

   Yes, he has.

2. _____ Taiwan?

   _____

3. _____ New Zealand?

   _____

4. _____ Japan?

   _____

5. _____ France?

   _____

B. What about you?

Complete the questions. Use *been, eaten,* or *seen*. Then write the answers.

1. _Have you ever been_ _____ to the United States?

   _____

2. _____ a kangaroo?

   _____

3. _____ cold spaghetti?

   _____

4. _____ to a museum?

   _____

5. _____ burritos?

   _____

6. _____ a llama?

   _____

C. Where have you been?

1. Write three places you have visited.

_____ _____

_____

2. Write three places you have never visited.

_____ _____

_____

3. Put them together to make sentences.

a. I've been to _____ , but I've never been to _____

b. _____

c. _____

D. What have you eaten?

1. Write three foods you have eaten.

_____ _____

_____

2. Write three foods you have never eaten.

_____ _____

_____

3. Put them together to make sentences.

a. _____

b. _____

c. _____

E. What have you seen?

1. Write three things you have seen.

_____ _____

_____

2. Write three things you have never seen.

_____ _____

_____

3. Put them together to make sentences.

a. _____

b. _____

c. _____

A. Match and connect.

fly •   • have stayed up

be •   • have used

go •   • have watched

stay up •   • have flown

bake •   • have baked

watch •   • have gone

use •   • have been

B. Fill in the blanks. Complete the crossword.

Across

1. drive   →   have _driven_____

2. _____   →   have slept

3. speak   →   have _____

4. write   →   have _____

5. ride   →   have _____

Down

1. visit   →   have _____

2. _____   →   have seen

3. read   →   have _____

C. Fill in the blanks. Answer the questions.

1. Have you ever _____ a comic book?

2. Have you ever _____ fishing?

_____

_____

3. Have you ever _____ a car?

4. Have you ever _____ a bicycle?

_____

_____

D. Fill in the blanks.

Use the words in the box to complete the questions for Janet.

flown	baked	written	been	stayed up	watched

1. Have you ever _____ cookies?   Yes, I have.

2. Have you ever_____ out of the country?   No, I haven't.

3. Have you ever _____ an English movie?   Yes, I have.

4. Have you ever _____ all night?   Yes, I have.

5. Have you ever_____ in a balloon?   No, I haven't.

6. Have you ever _____ to a pen pal?   No, I haven't.

E. Write questions and answers.

Look at Janet's answers above. Then write a question and answer for each one.

1. bake cookies

    Has she ever baked cookies?

    _____

2. watch an English movie

    _____

    _____

3. fly in a balloon

    _____

    _____

4. write to a pen pal

    _____

    _____

5. stay up all night

    _____

    _____

6. be out of the country

    _____

    _____

Let's Read

A. Fill in the blanks. Use the map of Paris.

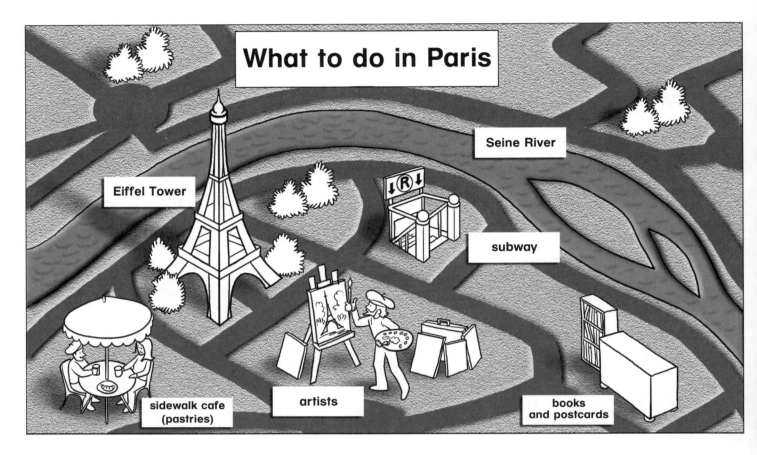

What to do in Paris

Seine River

Eiffel Tower

subway

sidewalk cafe (pastries)

artists

books and postcards

Eat breakfast outside at a _____. Try the _____. Go

for a walk along the _____ River. You can see many _____ painting

and selling their paintings. You can buy _____ and _____,

too. Don't forget to ride the _____ to the Eiffel Tower. The

_____ from the top is fantastic!

B. Match the cities and famous places.

1. Paris •   • Thames River, Regent's Park, Big Ben

2. London •   • Sumida River, Ueno Park, Tokyo Tower

3. New York •   • Hudson River, Central Park, Statue of Liberty

4. Tokyo •   • Seine River, Champ de Mars Park, Eiffel Tower

C. What about you?

1. Where do you live?

_____

2. Is there a river there?

_____

3. Is there a park there?

_____

4. Is there a tall building with a good view there? _____

D. Draw a map.
Make a map of your city. Then write three things to do.

1. _____

_____

2. _____

_____

3. _____

E. Find and circle the words.

| what | whale | whiskers | whisper | white | wren | wrap | wrench | wreath |

a	h	y	d	l	c	p	s	t	h	d	b	l	c	n	t	g	f	k
d	w	d	t	z	o	w	h	k	d	w	r	m	w	r	e	n	s	r
j	r	q	r	w	t	o	s	c	z	h	i	w	h	i	s	p	e	r
p	e	k	o	w	h	i	t	e	s	a	t	d	i	e	u	i	s	i
q	n	s	i	d	y	a	v	v	b	l	g	s	s	w	q	u	d	y
l	c	i	s	g	d	f	t	n	q	e	s	f	k	c	w	o	x	g
d	h	e	t	w	q	y	q	u	l	u	g	h	e	z	k	r	v	k
w	r	e	a	t	h	i	b	z	n	m	w	m	r	o	n	i	a	l
l	g	k	h	j	r	u	r	e	t	d	f	h	s	v	b	d	j	p

A. Do a questionnaire.

First answer the questions. Then ask a friend. Write *Yes* or *No* in the chart.

	You	Your Friend
1. Have you ever broken your arm or leg?		
2. Have you ever eaten a snail?		
3. Have you ever seen a penguin?		
4. Have you ever ridden a pony?		
5. Have you ever baked a cake?		
6. Have you ever watched a baseball game?		
7. Have you ever won a trophy?		
8. Have you ever flown an airplane?		

B. Think of four more questions.

1.		
2.		
3.		
4.		

C. Write five things you have never done.

1. I have never _____

2. _____

3. _____

4. _____

5. _____

Let's Listen

A. Make sentences about the chart.

Have you ever...	Craig	Sue	Mary	Brian
... been to an amusement park?	Yes	No	Yes	Yes
... broken your leg?	Yes	No	Yes	Yes
... been out of the country?	Yes	Yes	No	No
... ridden a motorcycle?	No	No	No	No
... flown in an airplane?	Yes	Yes	Yes	Yes
... gone camping?	Yes	Yes	No	Yes
... read an English book?	Yes	Yes	Yes	Yes
... watched a baseball game?	No	No	Yes	Yes
... spoken to a rock star?	Yes	No	No	No

1. Sue / baseball game

   Sue has never been to a baseball game.

2. Brian / amusement park

   _____

3. Mary / gone camping

   _____

4. Craig / rock star

   _____

B. Use the chart. Write questions and answers.

1. Mary / motorcycle _____

   _____

2. Craig / airplane _____

   _____

3. Brian / English book _____

   _____

Let's Review

A. Fill in the blanks.

1. Tim learned how to do a handstand when he was seven.

2. He learned how to write the alphabet _____

3. He started piano lessons _____ _____

4. He won a trophy when he was nine.

5. He started school when he was six.

6. He learned how to do a somersault _____

9 years old	
8 years old	started piano lessons
7 years old	
6 years old	
5 years old	learned how to write the alphabet
4 years old	learned how to do a somersault

B. Write the names and fill in the blanks.

When the school bus came...

1. Mike _____

2. Mark was playing with a yo-yo.

3. Nick and Katie _____

4. Jill was doing her homework.

5. Susie _____

_____ Mike Susie _____ Nick Katie

C. Match the questions and answers.

1. Have you ever eaten burritos? •   • No, I haven't. But I have broken my arm.

2. Have you ever seen a penguin? •   • Yes, I have. I stayed with an American family.

3. Have you ever broken your leg? •   • Yes, I have. I saw one at the zoo last summer.

4. Have you ever gone on a homestay? • • No, I haven't. But I have flown in an airplane.

5. Have you ever flown in a balloon? •   • Yes, I have. They're delicious!

D. Complete the sentences.

1. Dan has <u>flown in a balloon,</u>
   but he has never <u>flown in a</u>
   <u>plane.</u>

2. Mika _____
   _____
   _____

3. Ken _____
   _____
   _____

4. Todd _____
   _____
   _____

Read the questions and write a report. Draw a picture.

My Family and Me

What do you look like?

What do the other people in your family look like?

_____

_____

_____

_____

_____

_____

_____

Draw a picture.

My Favorite Activities

What do you like to do at school?
What do you like to do after school?
What do you like to do on the weekend?

_____

_____

_____

_____

_____

_____

_____

Draw a picture.

My Future

What do you want to be when you grow up? Why?
What will you do?

_____

_____

_____

_____

_____

_____

_____

Draw a picture.

More Review

My School Subjects

Which subjects do you like? Which subjects don't you like? Why or why not?

Which subjects are easy or hard for you?

What is your favorite subject?

_____

_____

_____

_____

_____

_____

_____

Write your school schedule.

My Favorite Season

What is your favorite season? Why?
What do you like to do?

_____

_____

_____

_____

_____

_____

_____

Draw a picture.

My Vacation

What did you do last year?

Who did you go with?

_____

_____

_____

_____

_____

_____

_____

Draw a picture.

My Next Vacation

Where are you going to go next year?
What are you going to do?

_____

_____

_____

_____

_____

_____

_____

Draw a picture.

More Review